A Mother's Love

LORI A. JONES

HERBET PUBLISHING

Edited by Vickie L. Tribble

Published by: HerBet Publishing

Book cover design by: Herbet Publishing

First edition: 2024

ISBN: 978-1-7327964-3-0

Printed in the United States of America

Dedication

This book is dedicated to my beautiful daughter, Kayla Miracle Hill. Kayla, you are my miracle from God, and I love you dearly. I know that there have been many times that I have been impatient and frustrated with not understanding some of the things we have encountered as mother and daughter. But never once in all of this have I regretted having you. Sometimes, my role as a mother has been unsure to me, but God has brought me a mighty long way, and I am grateful to him for that. Please forgive me for all the times I may have yelled at you because you did not know how to express yourself for some of your actions and did not detect when something was wrong. My prayer as a mother is for God to continue to teach me patience. Always remember that next to God, I love you more than words express. I pray that others will one day get an opportunity to know what a great young lady you are and touch many lives through God's grace.

Love,
Mama

Acknowledgments

First, I want to honor the Father, Son, and the Holy Spirit for keeping me through the years. Thank you for speaking through me to write this book and bringing every event back to my remembrance. I could not have made it without you being right there with me through it all. None of this would be possible without you. Thank you, Father.

I want to give a special thank you and shout-out to my beautiful Aunt Edna Cromartie. You drove me to the hospital, sat at my bedside, and helped take care of my babies any time I needed you. I am so forever thankful for an auntie like you. Love you.

My God-sister Jackie Reid Hunter, thank you so much for always being there to help pick up the slack with Alicia and PJ. Alicia loved always being with her Godmother, being spoiled every chance she could get. Thank you, my sister, for so much love.

A special thank you to my editor, Apostle Dr. Vickie Tribble. I met you 14 months ago at the Unapologetically Prophetic Conference 2023. I spoke to you briefly about needing an editor. You later became my spiritual sister with the Iron Tribe Network. When I reached out to you in February 2024, you saw the potential and were willing to assist when I had no idea what to do. You pushed me and educated me along the way. Thank you for setting a launch date and keeping me on schedule to meet it even when I felt burnt out. Through your inspiration and push, I will continue to write and birth out future books God has placed inside me. I can go forth now. I appreciate your patience as I continued to scribe as the Holy Spirit leads.

Love

Apostle Lori

Contents

Introduction

This story recounts the true-life events of my harrowing encounter with death while in premature labor during my third and final pregnancy. On Tuesday morning, November 27th, 2000, death came for me. I saw it approach my bedside, but I fought back and overcame it through the powerful name of Jesus. This was not Satan's last attempt on my life; he struck twice more. Once, I battled a severe fever, and another time, fluid accumulated in my lungs, making it hard to breathe. My medical team struggled to find a vein to start treatment. At one desperate moment, I prayed to God, asking Him to let me die so my unborn child might live. I felt I had lived a holy life before God and would make it to heaven. The marriage I was in made me feel like, "Lord, take my life." I was tired of what I was living in. However, God's plan was different. He intended for me, not anyone else, to nurture and love my child. God knew best. Who would take care of my children if I were gone? It was from my willingness to die for my daughter that I heard God speak to me and told me while lying there in the hospital to write a book about my journey of motherhood and entitled it "A Mother's Love."

If you read my story, you will find that, much like you, I am not exempt from life's hard tests and tribulations. Like countless mothers, I, too, have had to fight through the challenges of my child being premature and the complex health challenges that come with it. But it was not just the physical health challenges she experienced, but also the emotional challenges that occurred when my daughter had to cope with her parents' separation and inevitable divorce. Being a product of divorce was very traumatic for my daughter Kayla, causing her to experience significant behavior issues in her adolescent and preteen years.

As a parent, you try to protect your child as best you can from the trials that life brings, but as a mother, knowing that I was partly responsible for some of the challenges my daughter faced was heart-wrenching. As a mother, I had to confront those challenges by putting my faith and trust in God. During this time, God gave me a greater understanding of his love and grace. It was this same love God had showered on me that I learned the importance of having the capacity to show this same unconditional love to Kayla by not giving up on her during tough times. This agape love allowed me to continue being a role model and the disciplinarian I needed to be as a single parent. I hope my journey encourages and empowers you to continue to walk out your personal journey of parenting, knowing that in God's strength, you can provide a mother's love to your precious ones.

CHAPTER ONE

Unexpected Journey

My unexpected journey began in November 2000. I was the proud mother of two beautiful children, Alicia and Phillip (PJ). I was also pregnant with my third child, Kayla Miracle Hill, due in March 2001. Alicia was 11 years old then, and PJ was 15 months old. I was 25 weeks into my pregnancy with Kayla and was doing well. I had stressors going on in my life, like trying to salvage my marriage and keep my family together, all while working a full-time job for an optometry office. It was challenging, but I was working my way through it. However, my life drastically changed with one small, missed step. A few weeks before my pregnancy complications, I had a regular day. After work, I went to Aunt Edna's house to pick up

Alicia and PJ, who she babysat. While leaving her house, I missed the last step and fell, but I caught myself with my hands. I felt fine and did not think there was any harm done. My aunt suggested going to get checked out, but I had other things to do. Two weeks later, I noticed a liquid discharge, so I decided to see my healthcare provider just to be safe. They said everything looked good, and there was no leaking from the amniotic sac. However, as time passed, I realized everything was not okay.

My complications started on Black Friday in 2000. My Aunt Edna and I decided to go shopping. I had never been and decided I wanted to experience the great sales everybody talked about. We went out early and had a great time. We laughed and had so much fun. I began noticing I was getting a little cold. My throat started to hurt slightly, but I did not let that get the best of me. After we finished shopping, my Aunt Edna took me back home. I noticed I was getting chills at home and felt terrible as the evening progressed. To avoid coming down with something serious, I stayed in for the rest of the day and that entire Saturday.

The weekend seemed to pass quickly; before I knew it, Sunday morning, church time, was here. So naturally, I had to pull myself together and prepare for church. I was a choir member and had a song I was supposed to lead that morning. Truthfully, I was not feeling my best and did not know if I could sing, but I had to give it my all. When the time came for me to sing, I asked God to help me, and He did. I could feel the presence of the Holy Spirit on me like never before, and by his strength, I sang to the glory and honor of God. The congregation was blessed, and my soul was elevated. I remember the song's name was 'Jesus Will Work It Out. I had no idea that I was to sing my testimony and that God was preparing to do just that, work it out for me. God already knew the road set before me, and he knew how much I could handle. After singing and leaving the church, I was tired, so I went back home and got in bed with chills to follow. I woke up feeling awful Monday morning but had to go to work, so I went. The feeling of sickness stayed with me for most of my workday. It got to the point that I told my coworker that as soon as my workday was over, I was going to the pharmacist to see what I could take for what I had assumed was a bad cold.

It was about a half hour before quitting time when I started experiencing pain in my abdomen. It was contractions, and I was too early in my pregnancy to be having them. My other two children, Alicia and PJ, were overdue by two weeks and had to be taken by C-section, so this time around, I wanted to be educated and more aware of what was happening. I noticed that the contractions were coming about 10 minutes apart. I tried to remain calm and did my little breathing technique. When I finally got off work, I picked up dinner and went to the pharmacy. I asked the young lady at the counter if there was anything I could take for this cold, but was told that because I was pregnant, I should not take anything. I did not see the harm of taking something for a simple cold. The pharmacy specialist did not give any other reason than that. I left feeling frustrated because this cold was getting the best of me. So, I traveled to my aunt's home to pick up my children.

The contractions were still coming. I decided to call one of my dear friends, Emily Hall, a nurse. Who I felt could give me more insight than what the pharmacist advised. She said, "Lori, just go to the emergency room and have them check you out. It is not going to hurt anything, to be sure." I told her OKAY. Once I got to my aunt's house, I told her I needed to go to the emergency room and asked if she could take me. Teasingly, she said there was nothing wrong with me, that I just needed to go to the bathroom, but she agreed to take me. After deciding how to care for my other children while I was gone, we left her house and journeyed to the hospital. Once there, I went straight to the emergency room. I walked up to the window and informed the attendant that I was 25 weeks pregnant and having contractions. She immediately directed me to the admission counter. I have had experiences and heard many others talk about going to the emergency room and waiting hours to be seen. So, in my condition, I did not know what to expect. Thankfully, the hospital staff was on it concerning my situation. They understood the urgency and were acting on it, which, under the circumstances, gave me some ease and peace of mind. The ironic thing about all of this was, as I walked over to admission, there was a room full of pregnant women with their spouses or a significant one. I guess they were doing Lamaze class, and I looked like the one pregnant mom coming in late without her husband. The way they looked at me made me feel both hurt and ashamed. No, I was not there for their class, but I thought they were all wondering where my husband was. I was wondering the same thing. It was emotionally hurtful to see other women with their spouses with them. Yet, my husband was missing in action when I really needed him. But at that moment, I could not let that get to me. I had enough to deal with at that time. I shook it off and focused on what was happening in that instant.

I did not go sit with them. I proceeded to the admissions counter.

As soon as I reached the admissions counter, a contraction came. Before the woman in admissions could ask her first question, I held up a finger like we used to do in church before tipping out of the service. "Wait just a minute," I said, trying to regulate my breathing after the last contraction. Once I could speak, I told her, "I am 25 weeks pregnant and having contractions every 10 minutes." Those were the right buzzwords because immediately, I was directed to the labor and delivery section of the hospital. One of the staff brought a wheelchair; however, being that tough girl, I said, "That's alright, I'll walk." Back then, I tended to have a personality that didn't want to receive help from people. I call it being an independent woman. God calls it being prideful. Anyway, my aunt and I walked a long hallway to get to the elevators that took us up to labor and delivery. Lord knows I wished that I put my pride and independence in check and took the wheelchair because I was tired by the time we got to the labor and delivery area. We ran into the Lamaze group again as we got off the elevator. But by this time, my pride was gone, and in its place was both pain and distress. The director of the Lamaze group took one look at me, saw the distress on my face, and, without asking, came over and pointed us in the right direction.

Approaching the counter to let the receptionist know that I needed to be seen, but before I could, you guessed it, another contraction hit. Again, I lifted my pointer finger, "Wait just a minute, contractions, breathing time." The nurse came from the nurse's station and assisted me into a small room. When the nurse got me into the room, she had me go into the bathroom to undress and put on a gown. No sooner as I had put the gown on, I felt a gush of liquid come out of my body. Frightened, I screamed for help. My aunt and nurse rushed into the bathroom and helped me to get onto the bed. The realization that my water broke caused my eyes to widen with concern as I looked at my Aunt Edna.

I had not expected this at all. I was only 25 weeks pregnant, so my water should not be breaking. Things were happening too fast. The nurse immediately left the room, searching for the doctor. It was not long before the doctor came in and examined me. Then, after doing an ultrasound, the doctor was able to determine that my baby was in a breach position and was ready to come. I knew the situation was severe, and my baby's life was in jeopardy.

The doctor then informed me that their hospital was not equipped to help save my baby's life. At this point, not a single scripture came to mind. I was overcome with fear for my unborn baby's life. I couldn't grasp at what the doctor was saying or what and why all this was happening. When I got out of bed that morning, I knew I was not feeling the best, but how could things change from not feeling well to being in the emergency room with my baby, fighting for her life? I was going to the emergency room as a precaution for them to tell me everything was okay and that I was fighting off a bad cold. Now my water had broken, the doctor was saying my baby was breached, and to top that off, I was in labor.

Having been pregnant two other times with my other children, I knew that 25 weeks into this pregnancy, going into labor now was too soon, and there was a strong possibility that I was going to lose my baby or that my baby would have various complications. I wanted to put my clothes back on and find the nearest exit to get out of there. But even though I wanted to panic, I knew I was not in this alone. I felt God's grace come over me, and I could remain calm and brave. As the doctor again tried to explain what was going on, I listened as best I could as he gave the details of what he would do to try to prevent premature birth before they got me transported to the nearest hospital that specialized in premature pregnancies. My aunt Edna stood beside me, giving me all the comfort and support she could. At the same time, the nurse had already left the room to make the phone calls needed to transfer me to the other hospital.

In prepping me for the transport, the doctor gave me an injection of Nonsteroidal anti-inflammatory drugs (NSAIDs), Magnesium sulfate- which helps with brain growth in the fetus. I also received a round of antibiotics—to prevent or treat infection in me and my baby to help prevent premature birth. It did not take long for the medication to kick in because I immediately felt sick to my stomach. I felt my stomach flip-flop, so I turned towards my aunt sitting at my bedside. I said, "Get me something because I feel like I'm going to...." Before I could get all my words out, I threw up. My Aunt Edna quickly got me a bedpan. Still, unfortunately, she shared in the experience because, in the process, I spit on her too. When my stomach finally settled, she said, "Girl, you spit on me, and I'm going to get you." We both laughed, but we were laughing to keep from crying. We were terrified at the time because this wasn't what we expected. We sat together, engaging in small talk as we waited patiently for the arrival of the ambulance to transfer me to another hospital. We did not know what was happening. This was an unexpected journey, and we did not know how to respond.

When I think back on that day, my Aunt Edna will remind me that she has not forgotten that I spit on her and still plan to get back. Looking back now, I realize that the experience that day in the emergency room at the hospital and the staff was truly heartfelt and caring. Everyone was so genuinely caring and helpful to me. God took a terrifying moment in my life and, with great love and compassion, surrounded me with people who had empathy and were concerned about me and the wellbeing of my child and did all that they could to save us both. For this, I'll never forget and will be eternally grateful.

I was reminded of when God spoke to Joshua as Moses had died. Joshua was now in charge of leading God's people over Jordan. The scripture didn't say that Joshua was fearful as Moses had already trained him. But God reminds him of how he was with Moses, so he will be with him. So, if you are fearful, let me assure you. "*Have I not commanded thee? Be strong and of good courage; be not afraid, neither be thou dismayed: for the Lord thy God is with thee whithersoever thou go*" Joshua 1:9.

Life Lesson:

There will be times as an expecting mother, and even after birth, that fear will come to make you question or worry about what if something unforeseen happens. What will I do? If you begin to sit and allow your mind to worry with negative thoughts, you will give place for fear to take complete control. I encourage you to stay strong and know that God is with you. He has placed everything inside you to go through to birth and to raise the fruit of your womb. So, choose to laugh, as you can't afford to allow fear to get the upper hand.

CHAPTER TWO

Confusion in the Camp

T he ambulance had finally arrived to take me to the specialized hospital for premature deliveries. Aunt Edna had to return home to look after my other children and could not go with me. She promised that she would continue to try to contact my husband to inform him of what was going on and to get our children. Feeling uneasy about going alone, I asked the nurse if she intended to travel with me. She had been with me and my aunt the entire time, and to be honest, I wanted to have a familiar face by my side. A flood of relief washed over me when she said she would accompany me. It never feels good to be alone in an unfamiliar place, so even though this woman was a total stranger to me, the moment she said she would stay with me, I felt relieved and thankful for her kindness. Once in the ambulance, we were en route to the hospital. Noticing the surrounding silence, I asked the EMT if they had the sirens on. "No. Just the lights," they said. I had never been in an ambulance before, so I was terrified of what could happen to my baby if they didn't take me to the hospital immediately. In my head, I was screaming, "Don't you know this is a life-or-death situation? Everyone needs to get out of the way...get out the way!"

The entire situation was surreal and made me feel like I was in a Lifetime movie, which, by the way, I used to love watching throughout the week. I felt like the heroine being rushed to the hospital to save her baby. The ride was so long and shaky, and I could feel my contractions starting again. The nurse kept comforting me and assuring me that we would be there soon, and I prayed she was right. We arrived at the hospital at eleven o'clock during their shift change. I was quickly admitted to the hospital and placed in a private room. By this time, my contractions were strong, and I was in terrible pain. No one was in the room with me then, but I remember hearing many voices outside my room. It seemed as if the hospital staff were confused about how to deal with my case. It made me think of Exodus 32:17 when Moses went up to Mount

Sinai to receive the commandments from God, but on the way down, he could hear a bunch of noise and confusion in the camp. The staff were fussing about what someone did or did not do. At that point, I did not really care. All I knew was that I was in pain, my baby's life was on the line, and somebody had better get it together.

Finally, the doctor came into my room and introduced himself. He stated that he understood that I was 36 years old and wanted my tubes tied. I replied yes, not understanding what that had to do with what was happening to me and my baby at that moment. He then said to me in a dispassionate tone that because of the early contractions causing my premature labor, the baby would probably die, so was I sure that I wanted my tubes tied. The entire time he talked, I told myself, 'The devil is a liar.' I was scared for my unborn child but angry at the same time. How can a doctor stand there and say something like that with no compassion and provide no reassurance whatsoever? I responded with a yes regarding my tubes being tied but was unable to process the rest of his statement. With that acknowledgment, the doctor began to prepare himself to examine me.

Remember how I mentioned the confusion in the camp? Well, it turns out the doctor who was about to examine me was one of the voices I had heard earlier outside my room. I did not realize then that he was the doctor who had been upset about something before coming in. His examination was brutal. Whether he was still frustrated or just had a poor bedside manner, he pressed his hands so hard and deep into my womb that the pain was unbearable. The pressure was so intense that I started pushing my body up the bed until my head hit the headboard, trying to resist his force. In a contemptuous tone, he ordered the nurse to hold me still. My mind was scattered, but one thought kept coming back: 'Lord, this man is trying to kill my baby!' Already in pain, the doctor's rough examination only made it worse. What else could a terrified woman, who had just received the worst news possible, think then? All I could do was call on the name of Jesus repeatedly. After what seemed like forever, the doctor finally finished his exam and asked me again if I was sure about my tubes being tied. He informed me my infant would have at least a 75 percent survival chance if delivered. He went on to explain that by chance the baby did survive, there was a 50/50 chance the baby would be intellectually disabled or brain dead.

What was with this doctor and his negativity? I thought to myself, 'The devil is a liar, and yes, for the umpteenth time, I still want my tubes tied.' The doctor informed me that the baby was in position and ready to come. Surprised, I said, "I thought the baby was breached?" He replied, "No, the baby has turned into the correct position and is ready to come." He then explained that they could try to stop the delivery and give me a steroid shot to help develop the baby's lungs. However, I would have to lie flat on my back for two weeks because I was at high risk. This meant two weeks in the hospital, away from my two children at home. My husband, a high school teacher, and sports official was unreachable that night, which left me feeling uncertain. Despite the emotional turmoil, I knew I had to do whatever it took for my baby's survival. I decided to get the steroids to help build my baby's lungs and increase the chances of survival. The doctor administered the steroids, hoping this would improve my baby's chances of making it. By the time the doctor and nurse left the room, it was past midnight. I hardly slept that night, worrying about Alicia and PJ and how they would be taken care of. I was trying to figure everything out, wondering if my husband would manage their needs. I knew I could rely on my aunt if necessary. Scared and praying for my baby's survival, I was also anxious about what the doctor had said about the baby's potential lifestyle challenges. 'Lord,' I prayed, 'Can I handle this?' I don't know if I can. Please help me. God answered this simple prayer by reminding me of his word.

"There has no temptation taken you but such as is common to man: but God is faithful, who will not suffer you to be tempted above that ye are able; but will with the temptation also make a way to escape, that ye may be able to bear it," I Corinthians 10:13.

Even though this scripture did not apply to my current situation, I felt like, God, you know this is more than I can manage. I am going to need you to come through for me. I need a way out. I need you to show up. But I had to remember it was not in my strength but in God's strength.

The following day, I was not in any physical pain, but I was still emotionally concerned about Alicia and PJ. My experience with the on-call doctor that first night left me feeling dissatisfied with the level of care, especially compared to the previous hospital. When the nurse came in, I told her that I wasn't emotionally equipped to handle the doctor's negative bedside manner. His negativity affected my spirit, and I didn't want him to care for me. Already worried about staying in the hospital for two weeks while my other two children were at home, I didn't need any added stress from those who were supposed to care for me during this challenging and overwhelming time.

I don't know if the nurse relayed my message to the doctor, but his demeanor had changed when he came in for his rounds, as he was much more pleasant. I was surprised to see him but even more surprised by his improved attitude. I was glad I had spoken up. I never shared this with my husband or immediate family because I didn't want to create any unpleasantness, especially since my husband, a large man, could be intimidating. Since the doctor had improved, I decided to let it go.

Years later, God revealed to me that the doctor had repositioned the baby from breech to headfirst during that painful examination. What I had perceived as an attempt to harm the baby was, in fact, an effort to save her. The repositioning and administering of steroids were meant to buy more time for the baby's development. The Bible tells us to believe that God will direct us. Psalms 25:4-5 says, *"Show me your ways, Lord, teach me your paths. Lead me in thy truth and teach me: for thou art the God of my salvation; on thee do I wait all the day."* Thank you, God, for revealing this to me.

Life Lesson:

This experience taught me not to rush to conclusions. James 1:19-20 says, *"Wherefore, my beloved brethren, let every man be swift to hear, slow to speak, slow to wrath: for the wrath of man worketh not the righteousness of God."* Speaking, acting, or responding from a place of hurt can be misleading, as things are not always what they seem. Suppose I had relied on God's word during my difficult times instead of giving in to anger and accusations. In that case, the truth might have been revealed much sooner. Remember that God is a revealer of all things, even of things of the dark. *"He discovered deep things out of darkness, and bringeth out to light the shadow of death"* Job 12:22.

CHAPTER THREE

The Devil Thought He Had Me

All I could do was lie flat in bed, which I hadn't expected. These recent experiences had swung from one extreme to another, and now, to make matters worse, I couldn't even get up to go to the bathroom. The nurse had to help me use a bedpan. Seriously? This couldn't get any worse, or so I thought. I struggled to go while lying on my back with the pan under me, and with no success, I ended up needing a catheter. That wasn't pleasant, but I tried lighting the mood with humor to ease the stress.

My husband called when he could break away from class, but he couldn't come to the hospital. I asked him to call my mom to let her know I was there. He called her right after hanging up with me, and it didn't take long for her to call and check on me. I tried to explain the seriousness and risks of my pregnancy to her, including the need to stay in the hospital for two weeks to rest lying flat. My mom was concerned about the two other children at home and felt I could rest just as well there. She worried about who would take care of Alicia and PJ.

People may need to understand or realize that times are different now than when I was growing up. Not all families had the same upbringing. We were raised old school, as my generation would call it. This means that the majority of families believe in what the Bible and scripture teach: *"Train up a child in the way they should go, and when they are old, they will not depart from it."* Proverbs 22:6.

I must admit mothers, single and married. We are living in a world where so much goes on in homes. You don't know what is happening in other households and what is allowed and not allowed. Therefore, when you let your children stay out of the house so you can get a break, this lack of supervision may cause heartaches down the road. I'm grateful now for my uprising. I wasn't as pleased when I was coming up, but it didn't kill me. We had good manners and work ethics, and we respected our elders. In my mom's generation, you raised your own children. She and my dad had already raised us; back then, they didn't babysit other people's children. If you had children, you took care of them yourself. They didn't let their kids stay at everyone's house. But if I had explained better, her response would have been different. Even now, with Kayla as an adult, my mom is very protective of her and puts me in check if I seem too hard on Kayla due to her mood swings.

At that moment, I felt vulnerable, and it plunged me back into stress and worry. I have always been worried about what people thought of me. What would people think of me being away from my other two children for two weeks to rest? Really? The uncertainty of the situation and the lack of support put me in a bad headspace to the point where I began to feel depressed. I found myself unable to stop crying, and I didn't want to talk to anyone. Eventually, I remember drifting off to sleep. At least, I thought I was sleeping, but what happened next was real.

As I was drifting off to sleep, I remember looking down at my feet, and suddenly, a dark, bloody color shadow appeared at the foot of my bed and started moving up my body. As it traveled up my legs, a cold sensation began to pulsate over me as it moved closer towards my chest. I felt as if I were paralyzed and remember shaking while trying to open my eyes, but I couldn't. Instinctively, I knew this was the devil trying to take my life. I struggled to wake up, but I couldn't. In the natural, my eyes were closed, but my spirit was very much awake. As this demonic presence slowly crept up to my waist. I was in a panic because this event was so real, and I felt I was trapped and couldn't escape. But my spirit man refused to go down without a fight.

Suddenly, the Holy Spirit on the inside of me took control. The Lord knew it was not my time, at least not right then. I remember that chilling, dark presence reaching my chest. At that point, I knew the devil was too close for comfort. Any closer, and I believe the devil would have taken me out. But the God on the inside of me stood up, and before the enemy got to my neck, I screamed out, "Jesus!" Immediately, the demonic presence stopped. As fast as death came was as fast as it went. I could feel the presence recede from my body the way it came, and then it was gone.

I then opened my eyes. Hallelujah, Praise God. The name of Jesus is a powerful weapon against the enemy's attack. James 2:19 states that even demons believe that there is one God and tremble with fear.

I began to thank God for Jesus and my deliverance from the enemy's grasp. Glory, Hallelujah. As I opened my eyes, I looked at a picture on the wall in my room. It depicted a forest, and there seemed to be a person who appeared lost. Hovering over that person was a set of eyes high in the clouds, watching over them. At that moment, I felt God speak to my soul, assuring me that He was watching over me.

Admittedly, I didn't have my glasses on, so what I thought I was seeing wasn't part of the picture. For a moment, God had opened my spiritual eyes and allowed me to see what was happening to me in the spirit realm. How do I know? Because when I put my glasses on, all I saw were trees. God had allowed me to see myself in an unfamiliar place, but He was there to guide me through it. King David reassures us that there is no place where we find ourselves and that God is not there watching over us.

"If I ascend into heaven, thou art there: if I make my bed in hell, behold, thou are there. If I take the wings of the morning and dwell in the uttermost parts of the sea, even there shall thy hand lead me, and thy right hand shall hold me." Psalms 139:8-10.

On that day, God was right there in that dark place with me. Satan had waged war to take my life, but God blocked it. However, this was not my last encounter with the enemy during this journey.

Later that afternoon, a Perinatal Clinical Neuro Specialist visited to discuss coordinating resources, education, and emotional support. First, she had to explain her role to me, as I had no idea why she was there. The possibility of a premature delivery was frightening and often unexpected. The specialist provided me with educational material and discussed my job and whether I had FMLA. Since I had only been working at the optometry office for about 90 days, I had no available leave. I contacted my office to inform them of my hospitalization and current situation. Thank God for the practice owners—they were compassionate and family-oriented. They understood my situation, prayed for me, and encouraged me to take the time I needed, assuring me that my job would be secure.

This was a huge relief and reduced some of my stress. I watched some educational videos the specialist provided, knowing I needed all the information I could get for the challenging road ahead.

Later that evening, Tuesday, November 28th, I told the nurse on duty that the room was cold, and I was developing a sore throat from the air blowing on my head. I asked if I could be moved to another room since they had problems with the heating/air unit. Unfortunately, I ended up staying the rest of the night in that room, feeling myself getting sick all over again.

Life Lesson

When facing tests and trials, allowing your flesh to overpower your spirit opens the door for the enemy to wreak havoc. Even though my physical body was under attack, my spirit remained alert. 1 Corinthians 15:44 (KJV) tells us that we have both a natural and a spiritual body. Therefore, as a believer in the Lord Jesus Christ, remember to rely on your spirit in times of despair. The natural body can die, but the spiritual body cannot. The spiritual being can be quickened, enabling you to rise out of the enemy's grasp.

Chapter Four

My Decision

T he next day, they transferred me to another room. Later that evening, my husband finally arrived at the hospital. The doctors came in to discuss the possibility of having the baby naturally. I did not want to have the baby naturally and was very adamant about wanting a C-section. Some might wonder why I was so insistent on having a third C-section. Well given my past pregnancies and the counseling I received, it was a tough choice, but I opted for a C-section.

I was two weeks overdue when I was pregnant with Alicia, my oldest child. I was admitted to the hospital and induced into labor. A monitor was placed to listen to the baby's heart rate. My contractions were long and strong despite dilating to 2-3 cm. After hours of induced labor, the doctors detected a drop in the baby's heart rate, indicating distress. An ultrasound revealed that the umbilical cord was around her neck. An emergency C-section was performed, and she was delivered safely. It was terrifying to think that waiting could have cost her life.

With my son PJ, I was admitted to the hospital at 41 weeks. My first two children seemed to enjoy staying in my womb. They used a cervical ripening agent called Cervidil to help start the labor process, followed by Pitocin to augment the contractions. Despite six hours of a good labor pattern with Pitocin, I did not progress past 2-3 cm dilation. PJ remained very high in the pelvis and was in the left occiput posterior position, meaning his head was down but facing the front of me instead of the back. This made it difficult for him to move through the birth canal, leading to a diagnosis of cephalopelvic disproportion. This meant my pelvis was abnormally shaped and too small, the baby was not correctly positioned, and his head was too large.

The doctor discussed the risks of both a natural birth and a third C-section, considering the abnormalities of my pelvis and the potential complications of another incision in the same place. Although I wanted to deliver naturally, it would have been dangerous. I was taken to the operating room for a repeat cesarean section.

This was the reasoning behind my decisions. Having already undergone two C-sections, I knew a third would be risky. I felt trapped in a difficult situation—whether I chose a natural birth or a Cesarean, I was at risk. I believed attempting a natural delivery was too dangerous. My husband tried to persuade me to listen to the doctor, but it was my body and my decision. The doctor assured me that a natural delivery would be feasible given the baby's small size. However, I was resolute. I didn't even take the time to pray and consult God. I insisted they perform a C-section.

I had been unable to deliver my other two children naturally, and I wasn't willing to take a chance with this baby just because of the circumstances. Either way, the delivery would be dangerous and high-risk for both of us. I wanted my baby to have the best chance of survival, even if it meant risking my own life. I told my husband that I would rather our baby have a chance at life, even if it cost me mine. He was terribly upset by my talk of dying. I don't know what was going through my mind at the time; I just knew

I wanted my baby to live at any cost. I wasn't thinking about anything else. I had my chance in life, and my baby deserved hers. I felt, "God, take me and let her live."

After that conversation, the doctor left the room. My husband, realizing I wasn't listening to him or the doctors, decided to call someone he knew I would listen to. He phoned the church secretary, asking her to contact the pastor to talk some sense into me. He told her that I was talking about not wanting to live to save the baby. Even when the secretary tried to speak with me, I wouldn't listen. I believed I had lived a life pleasing to God and that if I died, I would go to heaven. I didn't understand God's plans for my life, so they earnestly prayed for me.

My family and church community lived over an hour away, so I didn't expect anyone to drive that far to sit with me and pray, especially since most of them had work commitments. I didn't have much to discuss with my husband; I had already decided and just wanted to rest. I had been there for only 2.5 days, dealing with one issue after another. What would two weeks be like? I just wanted to sleep. My husband went out to visit a friend he officiated basketball with who lived in the city we were in.

Later that night, I developed a fever. I called the nurse, feeling extremely cold and begging for covers and socks. The nurse took my temperature, and it was 101.6, which was considered high for me. My skin hurt due to the fever. The nurse said she couldn't give me any covers. The doctor ordered X-rays, and a specialist came to my room because I had to lie flat. The X-rays were challenging, especially when I had to hold my breath as I was struggling to breathe.

Shortly after the X-rays, my God-sister Jackie, Alicia, and PJ's godmother called to check on me and see if she needed to get the children. I was shivering badly but trying to hang in there. The doctor came in while I was still on the phone with Jackie and said I had fluid in my lungs and needed an IV to remove it. The nurse attempted to start the IV while I was talking to Jackie. When the nurse couldn't find a vein, I asked Jackie to call the evangelist and church mothers to pray. The nurse called for backup, and soon, I was surrounded by nurses and the doctor, trying to find a vein. I felt like I was going to die from all the needle sticks. Finally, a nurse tried the vein in my left hand, and it worked. I was bruised badly. Now, I always inform medical staff that the only vein that works is on my left hand to avoid unnecessary bruising.

As the IV was being set up, my condition worsened. The nurse said my facial color and lips had changed. I felt extremely weak and could barely lift my head. This felt like the devil's second attempt on my life. I looked up at a picture on the wall of people standing on a beach, watching someone far out in the water. It's amazing how God can take simple things around us to speak. I got my Bible and started reading the following scriptures.

"I waited patiently for the Lord, and he inclined unto me and heard my cry. He brought me out of a horrible pit, out of the miry clay, set my feet upon a rock, and established my goings. And he had put a new song in my mouth, even praise unto our God: many shall see it, and fear, and shall trust in the Lord." Psalm 40:1-3

"I shall not die but live and declare the works of the Lord." Psalm 118:17.

I was randomly reading from the Psalms to encourage myself. You might be thinking, isn't this the same woman who said she was willing to die for her baby? Yes, that's me. But God was working through it all, and my mindset shifted to believing that my God could come through. I felt my will to fight in prayer and with God's word growing stronger. I began to say, "In Jesus' name. In Jesus' name, the name above all names."

I took to heart what the scriptures were saying and called on the name of Jesus. As I said earlier, there is power when you call His name, and the devil trembles. At that moment, I remember coughing three times, and with the third cough, a thick mucus came out, and I immediately felt refreshed. Each cough represented the Holy Trinity: one for the Father, two for the Son, and three for the Holy Spirit. Good God Almighty, that's all it took. I began to say, Thank you, Jesus! Because I felt Him moving on my behalf, I was able to sit up in bed and put on my glasses and look at the picture on the wall. I saw that it was a lighthouse with people walking around, and one person stood out from everyone else. God told me that He was my lighthouse, watching over me.

This made me think of a lighthouse, which serves as an earthly example of a spiritual principle. A lighthouse is a tower built on shore or the seabed to aid maritime coastal navigation, warning mariners of hazards, establishing their position, and guiding them to their destinations. From the spiritual perspective:

"*Then spoke Jesus again unto them, saying, I am the light of the world: he that followed me shall not walk in darkness but shall have the light of life.*" John 8:12 (KJV)

"*The name of the Lord is a strong tower: the righteous runneth into it and is safe.*" Proverbs 18:10 (KJV)

God used these scriptures to assure me that He was guiding and protecting me through every aspect of my life and that everything would be all right. He then told me He wanted me to author this book and gave me the title A Mother's Love. He let me know that I had shown God's love by being willing to give up my life for my child. I said, "Yes, God, I will write the book. " But what is God's kind of love? The Greek word "agapao" or agape means unconditional love. This preferential love is chosen and acted out by the will. It is not based on the goodness of the beloved or on natural affinity or emotion. Instead, it is a benevolent love that always seeks the good of the beloved.

According to John 3:16-17, "*For God so loved the world, that he gave his only begotten Son, that whosoever believes in should not perish, but have everlasting life. God sent not his son into the world to condemn the world; but that the world through him might be saved.*"

Through the scriptures, God revealed the great love He had for me. Romans 5:6-8 says, *"For when we were without strength, Christ died for the ungodly. For scarcely for a righteous man will one die, yet peradventure for a good man some would even dare to do die. But God commended his love toward us, in that Christ died for us while we were yet sinners."*

"Who, being in the form of God, thought it not robbery to be equal with God: But made himself of no reputation, and took upon him the form of a servant, and was made in the likeness of men: and being found in fashion as a man, he humbled himself, and became obedient unto death, even the death of the cross." Philippians 2:6-8. Jesus loves us so much that He came, suffered, bled, died, and rose on the third day so that we may have life more abundantly. That's love.

Shortly after, the nurse returned to check on me and was astonished. She exclaimed, "Wow, you look so much better!" She noted that I had a glow compared to how I looked earlier. This was my chance to witness and share what God had done. I attributed the change to God's love for me. The saints were praying, and I called on the name of Jesus. I coughed three times, and in Jesus' name, a thick mucus came up, and I felt better. She was so happy for me. It was a time of praise and assurance that I would be all right.

God constantly revealed that He was right there with me, never leaving or forsaking me. I felt a profound sense of relief. Later that night, my husband returned and rested in the recliner. The nurse would come in periodically to check on me. Feeling completely exhausted, I tried to get a few hours of sleep. But anyone who has ever been in the hospital knows you don't really get too many hours of straight sleep without being awakened to see how you are doing. I'm sure I would have been much better if I could have gotten more sleep after all I had been through. Everything was going as the doctors had planned. The rapid changes I was experiencing were a lot to digest in just a few hours. But God was with me, so I did my best to get some rest.

Life Lesson:

I had to learn that making any decisions, especially as major as what I was dealing with, without consulting the Lord, is not what God desires from me or you. He wants to lead us down a sure path. God always wants what is best for us. Talk with God the Father as he has listening ears.

The scripture states, *"The Lord says, I will guide you along the best pathway for your life; I will advise you and watch over you."* Ps. 32:8 NLT. Allow him to direct your path.

CHAPTER FIVE

Ready or Not, Here I Come

I'm headed into three days now. Still, a lot has taken place, and I have 11 more days to lay flat in the hospital bed. It was November 30th, around 2:00AM, when the nurse came and checked my vitals. After she left, I hoped I would get to sleep for the rest of the night. But I felt something wet under my covers; figuring I might have wet the bed, I called for the nurse to let her know. When the nurse pulled back the covers to check me, she discovered my sheet was covered in blood. She immediately asked if I was having any contractions. I told her no. I hadn't had any contractions. In fact, I was resting well that night than

I had the previous night. Although they had the monitor on me, it wasn't picking up the contractions.

She hurriedly went to fetch the doctor. As I laid there, observing and pondering the situation, I optimistically assumed everything was proceeding smoothly. However, when the doctor arrived and examined me, he asked, "Are you experiencing any contractions?" Once again, I responded negatively, asserting, 'No, I'm not having any contractions.' To my dismay, he cautioned against pushing as the baby was imminently arriving. In a moment of distress, I inwardly protested as I dreaded the thought of her entering the birth canal. My faith, which typically provided solace, seemed distant and elusive in that instant. Despite the doctor and nurse's attempts to reassure me, stating, "The baby is small," and my husband's comforting words, "Everything will be alright, Lo," I struggled to find comfort amidst my escalating fear. It was evident that the medical team was mobilizing rapidly for this unexpectedly early delivery, and my mind raced with panic. The nurse urged me to remain calm and emphasized the importance of refraining from pushing, even though I lacked the sensation to prompt such action.

They swiftly transferred me to the labor and delivery room. With the assistance of my husband, I managed to climb onto the delivery table. The hospital staff hurriedly performed their preparations, given the situation's urgency. Unfortunately, there was no time for pain relief measures. When the doctor inquired if I was experiencing a contraction, I responded with a no. He then instructed me to push down, simulating a bowel movement. With two pushes, Miracle entered the world. In disbelief, I found myself questioning what had just transpired. Glancing to my right, I observed my newborn under the warming light, her delicate form appearing even smaller against the backdrop of the red heat lamps, which cast an unsettling hue upon her skin. Unlike the traditional bonding experience many mothers cherish upon their baby's birth, the immediate connection formed through holding their newborn for the first time outside the womb, I did not have the opportunity to experience with my precious Miracle. The nursing staff swiftly whisked her away to the prenatal care unit.

Miracle decided that she had plans of her own and made her grand entry into this great big world on November 30th, 2000, at 2:48 AM, weighing 1lb 9oz. She was so tiny that her dad held her in the palm of his hand. The nurse escorted me back to my room, where I could rest for the remainder of the night, or should I say early morning. It was truly astonishing how swiftly things had turned around. Initially concerned about a potential two-week hospital stay, God had orchestrated a remarkable transformation within just three days. The significance of the number three resonated once again, symbolizing the Holy Trinity of Father, Son, and Holy Spirit. His divine intervention left me in awe. Despite the early hours, I found myself wide awake. The nurse encouraged me to start moving around, and she kindly escorted me to the Neonatal Intensive Care Unit, NICU, to catch a glimpse of my Miracle through the glass. Seeing her fragile form filled me with gratitude and reverence. Thank you, Jesus, for your providence. It became evident that God had orchestrated events in a way that spared me from a third cesarean section. He instilled within me the strength to endure, even when doubt clouded my faith. What an omnipotent God we serve.

I had intended to breastfeed my Miracle just as I had done with my first two babies. However, due to her extreme prematurity and an Apgar score of 6 and 7 at one and five minutes, she would require NICU care until her actual due date. Kayla faced challenges with her breathing; her lungs were not sufficiently developed, resulting in

inadequate oxygen intake. It was heart-wrenching to con-
template leaving my baby in the hospital for four months.
Questions raced through my mind - "My God, what does
this all mean?" "Am I equipped to handle everything that's
unfolding?" I felt overwhelmed, wondering, "How much
more?" Was God testing my faith, urging me to trust Him
even in the face of uncertainty? I had no answers to these
questions. I had to do what Proverbs 3:5- 6 says: *"Trust
in the Lord with all your heart and lean not to your own
understanding in all of your ways acknowledge him and he
shall direct your path."*

My husband contacted my family—my mother, Aunt
Edna, and god-sister Jackie. They hurried to the hospital
that day to support me and see the baby. My mother was in
awe, exclaiming, "She's truly a miracle." Initially reluctant
to hold Kayla, Aunt Edna humorously likened her to a
cute little rat, showcasing her distinctive sense of humor.
They were all amazed by the small stature of this precious
blessing.

Amidst the turmoil and the challenges Kayla and I faced
over the past three days, I remained determined to have
my tubes tied before leaving the hospital. Yet, my hopes
were thwarted when I started to show signs of fever and

fluid in my lungs again. This complication meant that tubal ligation couldn't be done and had to be postponed. I felt frustrated, suspecting it was a ploy to charge more money. The doctor presented alternatives to my husband and me, proposing either a vasectomy for him or a Depo shot for me. My husband was hesitant to consent to the vasectomy at first but then decided to go ahead with the procedure. Later, my God sister Jackie came by, providing support and help with bathing. Once the doctors managed the fluid in my lungs, I was ready to go home.

Life Lesson:

We think we have everything figured out and know how things will play out. But God's knowledge and wisdom are far greater than man's. I was not expecting to have my miracle so quickly and naturally. I believe God was working on my behalf for my physical body. God had a purpose and plan. It all worked out for my good. As Romans 8:28 states, *"And we know that all things work together for good to them that love God, to them who are the called according to his purpose."*

"Be still and know that I am God." Psalm 46:10a. This is what God seeks from us. Don't obstruct His plans; in-

stead, move and flow with Him. He is the Master Teacher and Way-maker.

CHAPTER SIX

She's Coming Home

I was discharged from the hospital on December 2nd, just two days after giving birth. However, my Miracle, Kayla, would remain in the NICU for four months. The emotional turmoil began as I faced the reality of having to leave my baby behind. It was heartbreaking to part ways, and the distance added an extra layer of difficulty. Over an hour away, making daily visits impossible. Thankfully, arrangements were made by the Perinatal Clinical Neuro Specialist for me to stay at the Ronald McDonald House or return home. The Ronald McDonald House provided accommodation for families with seriously ill or injured children. Still, I couldn't stay permanently due to my responsibilities to my two other children at home. However, I was able to arrange weekend visits to be close to Kayla.

It was a challenging time, especially as I longed to nurse my baby as I had done with my other children. I craved that special bond between us, despite the tubes and wires that surrounded her. Determined not to let these obstacles hinder our connection, I returned home and attempted to pump breastmilk to take back to the hospital. Unfortunately, my efforts were hindered by poor eating habits and overwhelming worries about Kayla and the situation at home. The hour-long drive to the hospital made daily visits impractical, especially since my finances were tight and I had not yet returned to work. Nonetheless, I diligently called the hospital every day to check on my Miracle, even if it meant bombarding the nurses with my inquiries. Despite my efforts, I found myself sinking into sadness and struggling with postpartum depression, exacerbated by the absence of my baby by my side. However, I was touched by the generosity of others who supported me financially, allowing me to extend my stay with Kayla.

I was immensely grateful for the support of my Aunt Edna and god-sister Jackie, who lovingly cared for my other children while I focused on Kayla. Their willingness to step in meant that Alicia and PJ received extra love and attention, alleviating some of my worries. As time passed, I knew returning to work would limit my weekend visits, and I dreaded the day when this reality would hit. The journey ahead seemed daunting, but I found solace in the unwavering support of my loved ones and the knowledge that God was watching over us.

Everything that can be tested will be tested, and I mean everything. Trials and tribulations are an inevitable part of life, and there is no escaping them. However, during this critical phase in my daughter's life, I was inundated weekly with new obstacles to overcome. One particularly memorable challenge arose regarding the breast milk I prepared for my daughter. For those who remember the baby doll bottles from the '70s, you will recall their tiny size, not much larger than an average woman's pinky finger, with a plastic body and a little pink top. That was the size of Kayla's bottle - no bigger than my pinky finger. Due to her being so tiny, she could only tolerate about an ounce of milk per feeding delivered through tubes. Her body was so delicate that her little tummy could only accommodate small amounts at a time. Even her diaper, about the size of a standard yellow sticky note, emphasized her tiny stature. She was unbelievably small, a testament to her challenges from the beginning. One weekend, I diligently pumped bottles of milk to take to the unit. However, when I arrived and gave the nurse Kayla's bottles, the nurse questioned me, "Don't you already have milk here?" She then explained that the refrigerator had little room due to other babies' stored milk. I immediately felt a surge of frustration. "Who was she, the milk police?" I thought but managed to keep my composure outwardly. I couldn't help but wonder. However, with a touch of attitude, I calmly explained that I lived an hour away and could only bring what I could manage. She agreed to take the bottles that time but cautioned against bringing as much in the future. It was a test of patience, and I silently prayed for strength to maintain my composure.

During my visits to the NICU with Kayla, I faced another challenge. Strict precautions were in place due to the risk of infection, which required everyone to wash their hands meticulously and wear protective gear before entering the unit. Once inside, I would approach Kayla's incubator and observe her. The attending nurse would address her needs before leaving, while the escorting nurse would remain nearby. There was no opportunity to wander or socialize with other mothers; my focus was solely on my baby.

Seeing other mothers chatting and holding their babies only intensified my longing to hold Miracle. After a month of enduring this separation, I couldn't help but question why I was still facing such a trial. It felt like a test from God and weighed heavily on me. As a mother with a newborn, not being able to hold my daughter for an entire month took a toll on my emotions. I felt a whirlwind of feelings - sadness, frustration, and helplessness. Despite the urge to express my emotions, I had to maintain some level of composure.

Day after day, I would alternate between sitting and standing by Kayla's side, yearning to hold her. This routine persisted until one heartbreaking incident shook me to my core. During one visit, I reached out to touch Kayla's fingers, only to be reprimanded by a nurse. According to the nurse, touching Kayla would agitate her. Feeling a mix of hurt and anger, I left the hospital emotionally drained, seeking solace in tears at the Ronald McDonald House. Could I endure this trial any longer? A month had passed, and I still hadn't been able to touch my baby, let alone hold her. Amid my turmoil, I sought refuge in the kitchen eating, desperately seeking comfort amidst the storm of emotions.

My actual test came during a visit to my daughter when a nurse rubbed me the wrong way, nearly prompting a return to my old self. Before my conversion to Christianity, I had quite the mouth on me, filled with shameful profanity that I once found amusing. Thankfully, God delivered me from that, a fact I had to remember during this visit. I was sitting on the opposite side of Kayla's incubator, out of the nurse's view. The head nurse was sitting with me. As the nurse began checking on Kayla, Kayla became agitated, kicking vigorously. Inappropriately, the nurse remarked to the head nurse, "Look at her. I haven't even touched her, and she is kicking like a wild ***. " I'll let you fill in the blanks. The head nurse, recognizing the impropriety, shook her head to signal the nurse to stop. I stood up from behind the incubator in a flash, shooting darts at the nurse with my glare. Though saved, I am still a mother, and I couldn't bear to hear such heartless remarks about my daughter while she was fighting for her life. The nurse tried to be nice and play it off by saying, "She is a feisty little something, "Where did she get that from?" I looked her straight in her eyes and said, "My daughter's feistiness comes from her father, but don't mess with her mama." I never batted an eyelash. Despite my controlled demeanor, my eyes conveyed a lethal message. The nurse, realizing her misstep, quickly left. I sought out her name and spoke to the instructor, expressing my refusal to allow that nurse to be near my baby again. Though she was considered one of the best, I stood firm in my decision. I may not have raised my voice or cursed, but my eyes spoke volumes. I took a stand - sometimes, meekness can be mistaken for weakness, but I am anything but weak. I may be short, but I am a giant slayer, and anyone who dares to harm a mother's child is inviting trouble.

After enduring a month without being able to hold my baby, my time of testing finally bore fruit. A different nurse was attending Kayla's station, and something miraculous happened. Whether it was due to my previous report or the power of prayer, I chose to believe in the latter. Unlike the others, this nurse asked me if I wanted to hold my baby. I hesitated, recalling the previous nurses' warnings about agitating her. But the nurse assured me, "That's what your baby needs - to be wrapped in her mother's arms. " With trembling anticipation, I settled into the rocking chair as the nurse carefully placed Kayla in my arms. The joy that flooded my heart was indescribable. Even now, I cherish the photographs she took of that precious moment - the first time I held my baby in my arms. I began to sing to my precious one. I sang the song that most people know, but I changed the lyrics to fit just for Kayla. The song went:

I love you. I love you. I love you, Lord, today. Because you care for me in such a special way. That's why I'll praise you, I'll lift you up, and I'll magnify your name. That's why my heart is filled with praise.

My Kayla. My baby. My miracle from God. He sent you down to me and showed me all his love. And yes, I'll praise you, I'll lift you up, and I'll magnify your name. That's why my heart is filled with praise. That's why my heart is filled with praise.

Even after bringing Kayla home in the early years down the road, I would still sing that song to her. Sometimes, when she was acting a little irritated, I began to sing, I Love You, I love you, and immediately, she would stop what she was doing and look and listen. I knew that was a bond that connected us. As she got older, she would sing with me. Hallelujah. After holding my baby, things began to change after that day.

The doctors had to take Kayla to have surgery on her eyes because of so much oxygen going to her lungs. Her sight was being affected as well. But through it all, she began to gain a little weight. I was so happy because I held her more often and sang to her more. I could barely wait for the weekend so I could get to my baby. The hour drive was no longer a problem for me. It was all worth it. The time came for me to bring her a little outfit from home to put on. A pretty yellow jumper that my nurse friend and sister in the Lord Emilee had given her. Kayla was so cute in her outfit. Before we knew it, she was being transferred closer to home so she could soon be released. Once we got her to the local hospital, she was only 20 minutes away. I could see her every day. She was only there for 2 weeks. She weighed five pounds when she was ready to come home. It had been a long and trying journey, but now I could pour all my love into her at home with my Miracle. I still didn't know everything I would encounter once we got her home. But I was just so glad to be bringing my baby home. We bought Miracle home at the end of February 2001, which was earlier than the doctors expected, another miracle. As a mother, I can't fully express the joy I felt having my baby finally home. It was a long journey, but we made it to this place and were so grateful.

Life Lesson:

Having endured so many challenges to birth my miracle, I realized that God strengthened my heart during every test. I was able to be of good courage. The joy that went forth was only by God's hands. *"So be strong and courageous, all you who put your hope in the LORD,"* Psalms 31:24 NLT.

Conclusion

A s I set out to share my story, as directed by God, I was unsure how it would aid other mothers or those aspiring to motherhood. It was my personal journey and experiences—why would my story matter to anyone else? Over time, I grasped that our trials could act as a beacon for others, demonstrating that they, too, can surmount obstacles. The unforeseen complications during pregnancy are terrifying due to their unpredictable nature. Nevertheless, I urge all young mothers to believe in God—He will not disappoint you. All will turn out for their benefit.

It took years to realize this, but ultimately, everything will be fine. Trusting in God can alleviate stress and, to put it lightly, aid in maintaining youthfulness. I understood that regardless of the result, God had the optimal plan in mind. He anticipated the forthcoming challenges and equipped me with the grit and direction to face them, provided I relied on Him.

Being a devout Christian mother who frequented church every Sunday did not shield me from despair, anger, or the temptation to surrender. At one point, I even contemplated death. Life's harsh blows can provoke irrational thinking. My prayer for you is to never plead with God for your demise. Instead, pray, "Father, let Your will prevail, and grant me the strength to endure it." You can triumph over the most arduous periods through God's enduring support and a mother's affection. I could never have imagined handling Kayla's medical conditions and a marriage that fell apart. Still, I was sustained by God's love. Mothers, cherish your children and commit them to God—He will handle the rest.

Author's Note

T he journey to publish *A Mother's Love* has spanned 23 1/2 years, and my deepest hope is that it resonates with each reader. Although not all details are shared within these pages, my love for my daughter is immeasurable, beyond what she might ever fully understand or accept. This book is dedicated to inspiring mothers who may feel overwhelmed or tempted to give up when facing challenges. If you ever doubt your strength, remember that the Greater One lives within you, not in the world. Through Christ, who empowers you, you are capable of all things. You are ready for this journey.

Keep an eye out for the continuation of our story, detailing the challenges we faced after bringing Kayla Miracle home. At two years old, Kayla could only say "mama," "dada," and "eat eat." Her words were often jumbled together, making it difficult to understand her. It took an eye examination and glasses to bring her out of the darkness and help her speak clearly—a true miracle. One of our significant challenges involved dealing with the pediatric staff who administered a shot that caused Kayla's lungs to shut down, leading to a 14-day hospital stay. Her early childhood and adolescent years were filled with numerous challenges due to her premature birth. I had to make difficult decisions that took a toll on my health, but by the grace of God, we have made it through. So, look for part two of my miracle story coming soon.

You can reach Lori Jones on the following platforms:

- Email: LoriAJonesministries@outlook.com
- Instagram: @Lori.Jones.52459
- Facebook: @Lori Ann Jones
- Website: [www.IAMLORIJONES.com](http://www.iamlorijones.com)

Made in the USA
Columbia, SC
13 August 2024

39950029R00039